INSIDE THE NHL

Winnipeg Jets

Ramey Temple

AV2 BY WEIGL
MEDIA ENHANCED BOOKS
ADDED VALUE • AUDIO VISUAL

www.av2books.com

MEDIA ENHANCED BOOKS
AV²
BY WEIGL™
ADDED VALUE • AUDIO VISUAL

AV² provides enriched content that supplements and complements this book. Weigl's AV² books strive to create inspired learning and engage young minds in a total learning experience.

Your AV² Media Enhanced books come alive with...

Audio
Listen to sections of the book read aloud.

Key Words
Study vocabulary, and complete a matching word activity.

Video
Watch informative video clips.

Quizzes
Test your knowledge.

Embedded Weblinks
Gain additional information for research.

Slide Show
View images and captions, and prepare a presentation.

Go to **www.av2books.com**, and enter this book's unique code.

BOOK CODE

W552946

AV² by Weigl brings you media enhanced books that support active learning.

Try This!
Complete activities and hands-on experiments.

... and much, much more!

Published by AV² by Weigl
350 5ᵗʰ Avenue, 59ᵗʰ Floor
New York, NY 10118
Websites: www.av2books.com   www.weigl.com

Library of Congress Control Number: 2014951855

ISBN 978-1-4896-3197-8 (hardcover)
ISBN 978-1-4896-4020-8 (softcover)
ISBN 978-1-4896-3198-5 (single-user eBook)
ISBN 978-1-4896-3199-2 (multi-user eBook)

Printed in the United States of America in Brainerd, Minnesota
1 2 3 4 5 6 7 8 9 0 19 18 17 16 15

032015
WEP050315

Senior Editor Heather Kissock
Art Director Terry Paulhus

Photo Credits
Every reasonable effort has been made to trace ownership and to obtain permission to reprint copyright material. The publishers would be pleased to have any errors or omissions brought to their attention so that they may be corrected in subsequent printings.

Weigl acknowledges Getty Images and iStock as its primary image suppliers for this title.

Winnipeg Jets

CONTENTS

Introduction

The Winnipeg Jets have a long and storied history with the city of Winnipeg. The team officially began play in 1979, but 16 years later was moved to Phoenix and renamed the Coyotes. Although some Jets fans continued to follow the Coyotes in the desert, many felt like they had lost their team for good. That all changed in 2011, when the Atlanta Thrashers were moved north to the city of Winnipeg. The Thrashers were immediately renamed the Winnipeg Jets.

The Jets have not qualified for the postseason since moving back to Winnipeg in 2011. Up and coming young players such as Mark Scheifele hope to change that.

The original Jets had 11 **playoff** appearances during 16 seasons, but never experienced Stanley Cup glory. During the **franchise's** 11 seasons in Atlanta, they only reached the playoffs once, back in 2007. In many ways, the restart in Winnipeg represents a new beginning as the franchise aims to write their own history behind a talented and exciting group of young players.

Winnipeg JETS

Arena	MTS Centre
Division	Central
Head Coach	Paul Maurice
Location	Winnipeg, Manitoba
NHL Stanley Cup Titles	None
Nicknames	The Jets

Andrew Ladd is the current captain of the Jets. A veteran and a champion, Ladd will be counted on for leadership and his play making ability.

12
Playoff
appearances

3
Calder
trophies

5
Hall
of Famers

History

The Jets have posted **WINNING RECORDS** in all three seasons since relocating to Winnipeg, narrowly missing the playoffs each time.

The 2011–2012 Winnipeg Jets won 37 games. In the 2013–2014 season, the team also won 37 games.

The original Winnipeg Jets joined the National Hockey League (NHL) in 1979 after playing in the **World Hockey Association (WHA)** for seven seasons. The team played for 16 NHL seasons as the Jets before they ran into some financial trouble. Despite efforts by Winnipeg residents to keep the team, the new owners moved the Jets to Phoenix in 1996 and changed their name to the Coyotes. The Jets played what they thought was their last game in Winnipeg on April 28, 1996.

Three years later, the NHL expanded, and a new franchise called the Atlanta Thrashers began. Many thought ice hockey in the state of Georgia was a strange experiment. Over the next 11 seasons, the Thrashers never quite settled down in Atlanta, only qualifying for the playoffs once.

In 2011, to the delight of a passionate Canadian fan base up north, the Thrashers were moved to Winnipeg to play in front of packed houses nightly at the MTS Centre. These new Jets play in the Western Conference's Central Division and share a complex history with the original Jets (1979–1996), the Thrashers (1999–2011), and the current Arizona Coyotes (1996–present).

Despite an unfamiliar new team design, and 15 seasons without NHL hockey, Winnipeg residents were proud to once again wave the banner for their beloved Jets.

The Arena

In terms of seating capacity, MTS Centre is the smallest venue in the NHL. Despite this, the arena is filled to capacity with avid Jets fans nearly every night.

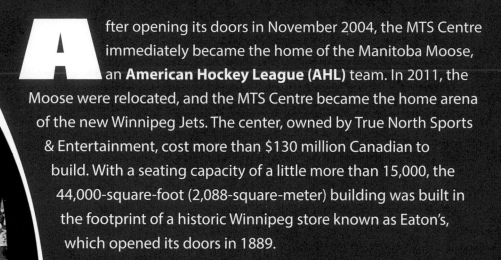

After opening its doors in November 2004, the MTS Centre immediately became the home of the Manitoba Moose, an **American Hockey League (AHL)** team. In 2011, the Moose were relocated, and the MTS Centre became the home arena of the new Winnipeg Jets. The center, owned by True North Sports & Entertainment, cost more than $130 million Canadian to build. With a seating capacity of a little more than 15,000, the 44,000-square-foot (2,088-square-meter) building was built in the footprint of a historic Winnipeg store known as Eaton's, which opened its doors in 1889.

There are plans in place to modernize the arena and the surrounding downtown area over the next six years. The goal is to build downtown Winnipeg up, with the Jets arena at the center of it all. The new downtown will be a place where fans can socialize and eat before heading to the Jets game or other events taking place at the MTS Centre. Over the past few years, in addition to selling out for Jets hockey games, the center has hosted high-profile concerts by performers such as Bon Jovi and Metallica.

Stacey Nattrasss has been the Jets' national anthem singer since 2011.

Where They Play

British Columbia

Alberta

CANADA

Saskatchewan

Manitoba

Ontario

4

3

7

★ **14** MTS Centre, Winnipeg

Washington

Montana

North Dakota

Minnesota

11

Wisconsin

8

Oregon

Idaho

South Dakota

UNITED

Iowa

Illinois

Wyoming

Nebraska

STATES

Nevada

Utah

Colorado

Kansas

Missouri

13

9

6

California

5

Arizona

New Mexico

Oklahoma

Arkansas

1

2

MEXICO

Texas

10

Louisiana

Missis.

Pacific Ocean

Gulf of Mexico

NHL WESTERN CONFERENCE

PACIFIC DIVISION

1 Anaheim Ducks
2 Arizona Coyotes
3 Calgary Flames
4 Edmonton Oilers
5 Los Angeles Kings
6 San Jose Sharks
7 Vancouver Canucks

CENTRAL DIVISION

8 Chicago Blackhawks
9 Colorado Avalanche
10 Dallas Stars
11 Minnesota Wild
12 Nashville Predators
13 St. Louis Blues
★ 14 Winnipeg Jets

MTS centre

Arena
MTS Centre

Location
300 Portage Ave.
Winnipeg, MB R3C 5S4

Broke Ground
April 16, 2003

Completed
November 16, 2004

Features
• capacity for 16,000 concertgoers,
  15,000 hockey fans
• four Skywalk links
• traditional red brick architecture
• private party suites

LEGEND
☆ MTS Centre
■ Eastern Conference
■ Western Conference

Newfoundland

Quebec

Prince Edward Island

New Brunswick

New Hampshire

Vermont

Maine

20

Nova Scotia

19

15 Massachusetts

22

26

Rhode Island

27

Connecticut

17

New York

25

Michigan

16

New Jersey

Pennsylvania

29

Ohio

28

Indiana

24

30

West Virginia Virginia

Delaware

Maryland

District of Columbia

Kentucky

23

North Carolina

Tennessee

12

South Carolina

Alabama

Georgia

Atlantic Ocean

Florida

21

18

issippi

ATLANTIC DIVISION

15	Boston Bruins	19	Montreal Canadiens
16	Buffalo Sabres	20	Ottawa Senators
17	Detroit Red Wings	21	Tampa Bay Lightning
18	Florida Panthers	22	Toronto Maple Leafs

METROPOLITAN DIVISION

23	Carolina Hurricanes	27	New York Rangers
24	Columbus Blue Jackets	28	Philadelphia Flyers
25	New Jersey Devils	29	Pittsburgh Penguins
26	New York Islanders	30	Washington Capitals

Winnipeg Jets   **11**

The Uniforms

9 Bobby Hull's number 9 was retired by the original Jets franchise in Winnipeg. When the Jets moved back to Winnipeg, Hull allowed the team to use his old number.

The Jets' team symbol appears on the shoulders of both the home and away jerseys.

The new Jets uniforms pay respect to the original Jets with a color scheme of dark blue, light blue, silver, and white. The new **logo** is a picture of a fighter jet hovering over a Canadian maple leaf symbol, which honors the Royal Canadian Air Force. This logo appears in the center of the jersey and is a departure from the original Jets logos, which featured a hockey stick as the letter "J" in Jets.

HOME

Unlike on the old Jets uniforms, the Canadian maple leaf is the only aspect of the jersey that is red. The home jerseys are dark blue with white and light blue striping. The away jersey is white with two shades of blue striping. Both are worn with dark blue pants.

AWAY

The Jets have not made any changes to their uniforms since the team arrived back in Winnipeg in 2011.

Helmets and Face Masks

1 The Jets have only had one helmet design since moving back to Winnipeg in 2011.

The Jets recently added a "Hockey Fights Cancer" sticker to their home and away helmets to help raise awareness about the deadly disease.

The Jets helmets are dark blue or white, depending on the type of jersey the player is wearing, and do not have the team logo printed on them. Due to the danger of head injuries that go along with playing their position, goaltenders wear helmets that are larger than those used by position players. The larger helmets also mean there is more blank space for goalies to be creative with their personal artwork and designs. The decorating of goalie helmets has become a true art form for NHL players.

Ondrej Pavelec, a goalie for the Jets, decorated his helmet with the team logo on the front, flying jet patterns on the side, and an iron shark character on the chin. The helmet is mostly silver, although the face mask has a hint of gold on it. There are also Canadian maple leaves on both sides of Pavelec's helmet, which represent Winnipeg's Canadian pride.

Pavelec chose to place a shark on the area below his chin on his helmet to represent the way he attacks defenders who are trying to score.

The Coaches

4 Paul Maurice has been the head coach for four different NHL teams.

Paul Maurice has coached one team to the conference finals and another to the Stanley Cup Final in his career. The next step would be a title during his time in Winnipeg.

The Jets have had several great coaches who each had a hand in leading the team through a complicated transition from Atlanta to Winnipeg. These men have worked hard to reestablish the great hockey tradition in the city of Winnipeg with today's Jets. Claude Noel and Paul Maurice are the two most recent coaches for the new Jets. Each has helped position these young Jets for a run at the Stanley Cup.

CLAUDE NOEL The year before the Thrashers came to Winnipeg and became the Jets, Claude Noel had been coaching the Manitoba Moose of the AHL. He became the first head coach of the Jets after they moved to Winnipeg to start the 2011 season. The team he took over had finished with a mediocre 34–36–12 record the year prior, playing as the Atlanta Thrashers. The Jets improved in Noel's first season, winning 37 games, 23 of them at the MTS Centre.

PAUL MAURICE Paul Maurice is the current coach of the Jets. He previously coached the Carolina Hurricanes, Hartford Whalers, and Toronto Maple Leafs. Maurice earned a career-high 40 wins with Toronto during the 2006–2007 season, and has almost 500 wins in his coaching career. The Jets hope that his experience will rub off on their young and talented team.

Fans and the Internet

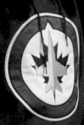
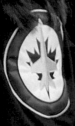

Jets fans come to the MTS Centre prepared to cheer on the home team, often wearing their favorite player's jersey, holding team banners, and participating in group cheers.

The Jets have their own NHL website, www.jets.nhl.com, where fans can buy tickets, visit their team store, access statistics, interact in a fan zone, and even play fantasy hockey. The site is also linked to social media outlets, including Instagram, Facebook, and Twitter. Many fans follow their favorite Jets players on the players' personal Twitter accounts.

Despite the Jets' limited recent team history, they have thousands of followers online, many of whom read about the Jets on the three very popular team blogs. Websites such as Arctic Ice Hockey, arcticicehockey.com, JetsNation, www.jetsnation.ca, and Illegal Curve, www.illegalcurve.com, pick up where the official NHL website leaves off. These blogs allow fans to communicate and discuss the Jets in an open forum.

Signs
of a fan

#1 The tradition of fans wearing all white to Jets playoff games began in 1987. Now known as the Winnipeg White Out, this tradition began as a response to Calgary Flames fans, who wore all red in the first round of the playoffs.

#2 The Jets Cadet Kids Club offers young members exclusive tickets to special events as well as awesome games and prizes.

Legends of the Past

Many great players have suited up for the Jets. A few of them have become icons of the team and the city it represents.

Teemu Selanne

Nicknamed the "Finnish Flash" because of his legendary speed on the ice, Teemu Selanne is a native of Finland who enjoyed a tremendous 21-year NHL career. He announced his arrival with an exclamation mark during his **rookie** season in Winnipeg. He collected an amazing 132 points that season, setting an NHL rookie record for goals, with 76. Hockey experts consider this one of the greatest NHL seasons ever. Selanne's early success set the stage for a long and storied career that followed.

Position: Right Wing
NHL Seasons: 21 (1992–2014)
Born: July 3, 1970, in Helsinki, Finland

Dale Hawerchuk

After playing his first NHL game at the age of 18, Dale "Ducky" Hawerchuk did not take long to become a Winnipeg Jets legend. In 1981, the rookie play-making center led the Jets to the largest one-year turnaround in NHL history, a 48-point improvement. He also became the youngest NHL player to reach the 100-point mark in NHL history that season, and was awarded the Calder Memorial Trophy as the Rookie of the Year. The five-time **All-Star** scored more than 100 points in six of his nine seasons in Winnipeg. When he was traded in 1989, Hawerchuk left the Jets holding 17 club records.

Position: Center
NHL Seasons: 16 (1981–1997)
Born: April 4, 1963, Toronto, Ontario, Canada

Paul MacLean

Paul MacLean was drafted by the St. Louis Blues in 1980, but only played one game for them. MacLean was known for being a sharpshooter and an offensive player who was not afraid to play defense. He was quickly traded to the Jets in what turned out to be one of the greatest trades in franchise history. MacLean would go on to score 248 goals and record 270 **assists** over seven seasons, playing alongside Dale Hawerchuk on a very productive **line**. MacLean currently is the head coach of the Ottawa Senators.

Position: Right Wing
NHL Seasons: 11 (1980–1991)
Born: March 9, 1958, in Grostenquin, France

Stars of Today

Today's Jets team is made up of many young, talented players who have proven that they are among the best in the league.

Dustin Byfuglien

Dustin Byfuglien began playing in the NHL in 2003. He then played five seasons for the Chicago Blackhawks before being traded to the Atlanta Thrashers in 2010, where he made his first All-Star appearance. Byfuglien moved to Winnipeg in 2011 when the team changed cities, and remained just as productive. He was selected as an All-Star in the 2011 and 2012 seasons. At 6 feet 5 inches (2 meters) tall and weighing more than 260 pounds (118 kilograms), the skilled defenseman is an intimidating force.

Position: Right Wing/Defenseman
NHL Seasons: 10 (2005–Present)
Born: March 27, 1985, in Minneapolis, Minnesota, United States

Andrew Ladd

At 6 feet 3 inches (1.9 m) tall, Andrew Ladd is a big left wing who plays the game fast and can score the puck. Ladd is a proven winner, having won the Stanley Cup with the Carolina Hurricanes in 2005, and again with the Chicago Blackhawks in 2010. The season following his second trip to the Stanley Cup Final, he was traded to the Thrashers. After one year in Atlanta, he found himself headed to Winnipeg, where he hopes his playoff experience will rub off on his new teammates.

Position: Left Wing
NHL Seasons: 10 (2005–Present)
Born: December 12, 1985, in Maple Ridge, British Columbia, Canada

Blake Wheeler

Blake Wheeler began his career in 2004 as the fifth overall pick of the Phoenix Coyotes, but never played a single game with them. He eventually signed with the Boston Bruins, but was traded in the middle of the 2010 season to the Thrashers. When the team moved to Winnipeg, something clicked for Wheeler. His game seemed to steadily improve in Winnipeg. In 2013–2014, Wheeler scored 28 goals and had 41 assists. He is a large wing and is at his best when driving through traffic near the net.

Position: Right Wing
NHL Seasons: 7 (2008–Present)
Born: August 31, 1986, in Robbinsdale, Minnesota, United States

All-Time Records

5 Seconds
Fastest Goal in NHL History
Original Jets player Doug Smail scored one of the fastest goals in NHL history, just five seconds after the opening face-off.

9
Most Goals from different players
In one wild game in 2011, the Jets scored nine goals from nine different players to beat the Philadelphia Flyers, setting a franchise record in the process.

76
Most Goals at 22
Teemu Selanne proved to be one of the best rookies in NHL history, scoring 76 goals in the 1992 season, at just 22 years of age.

291
Active Points Leader
Entering the 2014–2015 season, Bryan Little topped the points list for active Jets players, with 291.

AWARENESS

79
Most assists in a single season
Phil Housley has the all-time Jets single-season record for assists, with 79 in 1992.

Timeline

Throughout the team's history, the Winnipeg Jets have had many memorable events that have become defining moments for the team and its fans.

1972
The Jets begin play in the World Hockey Association. The league would close seven years later.

1979
The Jets are added as an **expansion** team in the NHL.

| 1965 | 1970 | 1975 | 1980 | 1985 | 1990 |

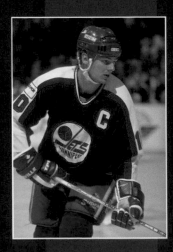

In 1981, the Jets sign Dale Hawerchuk, who proves to be one of the greatest players in Jets history. In his first season, Hawerchuk breaks the 100-point mark and wins the Calder Memorial Trophy.

1985
The Calgary Flames defeat the Jets during the playoffs in three games. The Jets finish third that season in the Smythe Division.

The Future

The Jets have had a long and complicated history from Winnipeg to Phoenix, and then from Atlanta to Winnipeg. In fact, the Jets have two distinct team histories, spanning four cities. The future, however, is all about their talented young team and being reunited with the city of Winnipeg. The fans never stopped loving their Jets, and are thrilled to have them back. The next step is to start another winning tradition and to bring home the first Stanley Cup to Winnipeg.

1992

Teemu Selanne makes his record-breaking debut with 76 goals and 132 points as a rookie Jets player. The Jets finish in fourth place overall.

In 2011, the Thrashers move to Winnipeg, where the franchise becomes the Winnipeg Jets.

| 1995 | 2000 | 2005 | 2010 | 2015 | 2020 |

2014

The 2013–2014 season marks the Jets third straight winning season since reuniting with the city of Winnipeg.

1996

The Jets franchise is moved to Phoenix, Arizona, where the team is renamed the Coyotes.

Write a Biography

Life Story

A person's life story can be the subject of a book. This kind of book is called a biography. Biographies often describe the lives of people who have achieved great success. These people may be alive today, or they may have lived many years ago. Reading a biography can help you learn more about a great person.

Get the Facts

Use this book, and research in the library and on the internet, to find out more about your favorite Jet. Learn as much about this player as you can. What position does he play? What are his statistics in important categories? Has he set any records? Also, be sure to write down key events in the person's life. What was his childhood like? What has he accomplished off the field? Is there anything else that makes this person special or unusual?

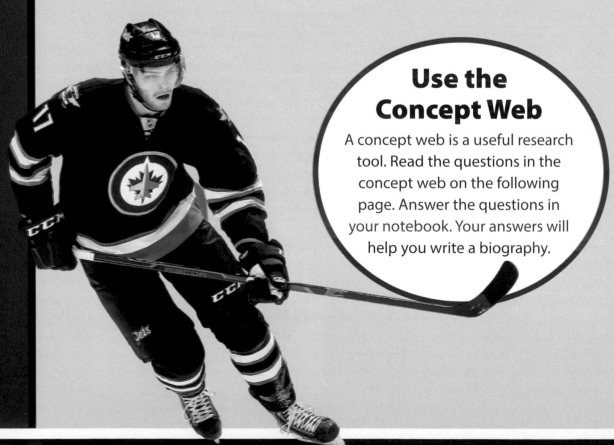

Use the Concept Web

A concept web is a useful research tool. Read the questions in the concept web on the following page. Answer the questions in your notebook. Your answers will help you write a biography.

Concept Web

Adulthood
- Where does this individual currently reside?
- Does he or she have a family?

Your Opinion
- What did you learn from the books you read in your research?
- Would you suggest these books to others?
- Was anything missing from these books?

Childhood
- Where and when was this person born?
- Describe his or her parents, siblings, and friends.
- Did this person grow up in unusual circumstances?

Accomplishments off the Field
- What is this person's life's work?
- Has he or she received awards or recognition for accomplishments?
- How have this person's accomplishments served others?

Write a Biography

Help and Obstacles
- Did this individual have a positive attitude?
- Did he or she receive help from others?
- Did this person have a mentor?
- Did this person face any hardships?
- If so, how were the hardships overcome?

Accomplishments on the Field
- What records does this person hold?
- What key games and plays have defined his career?
- What are his stats in categories important to his position?

Work and Preparation
- What was this person's education?
- What was his or her work experience?
- How does this person work?
- What is the process he or she uses?

Trivia Time

Take this quiz to test your knowledge of the Winnipeg Jets. The answers are printed upside down under each question.

1 Which Jets player has won two Stanley Cups with the Carolina Hurricanes and Chicago Blackhawks?

A. Andrew Ladd

2 Who is the current coach of the Jets?

A. Paul Maurice

3 In what division do the Jets play?

A. Central Division

4 What is the name of the Jets' current arena?

A. MTS Centre

5 What is Dale Hawerchuk's nickname?

A. "Ducky"

6 What city did the Jets play in before moving to Winnipeg?

A. Atlanta

7 In what year did the Jets return to Winnipeg?

A. 2011

8 After leaving Winnipeg in 1995, what city did the franchise move to?

A. Phoenix

9 What image is on the Jets' current logo?

A. A fighter jet

Key Words

All-Star: a game made for the best-ranked players in the NHL that happens mid-season. A player can be named an All-Star and then be sent to play in this game.

American Hockey League (AHL): a hockey league based in America and Canada where players develop skills until they are ready for the NHL

assists: a statistic that is attributed to up to two players of the scoring team who shoot, pass, or deflect the puck toward the scoring teammate

expansion: expansion in the NHL is marked by the addition of a new franchise. The league last expanded in 2000 when the Columbus Blue Jackets and Minnesota Wild joined the NHL.

franchise: a team that is a member of a professional sports league

line: forwards who play in a group, or "shift," during a game

logo: a symbol that stands for a team or organization

playoff: a series of games that occur after regular season play

rookie: a player age 26 or younger who has played no more than 25 games in a previous season, nor six or more games in two previous seasons

World Hockey Association (WHA): the North American professional hockey league that merged with the NHL in 1979

Index

Log on to www.av2books.com

AV² by Weigl brings you media enhanced books that support active learning. Go to www.av2books.com, and enter the special code found on page 2 of this book. You will gain access to enriched and enhanced content that supplements and complements this book. Content includes video, audio, weblinks, quizzes, a slide show, and activities.

AV² Online Navigation

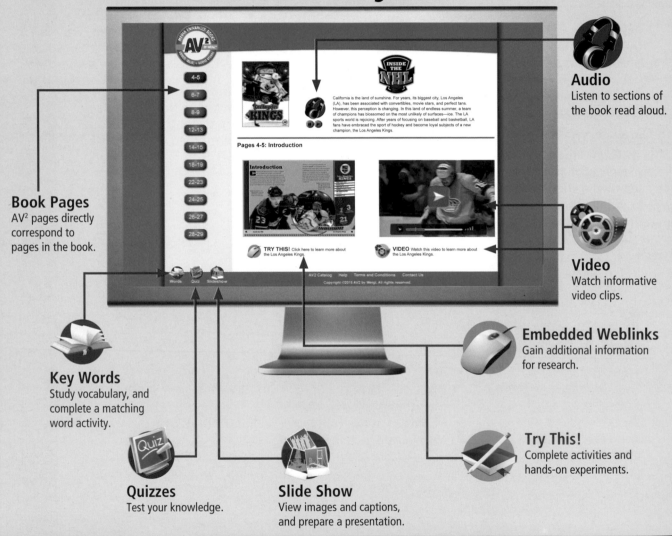

Audio
Listen to sections of the book read aloud.

Book Pages
AV² pages directly correspond to pages in the book.

Video
Watch informative video clips.

Key Words
Study vocabulary, and complete a matching word activity.

Embedded Weblinks
Gain additional information for research.

Quizzes
Test your knowledge.

Slide Show
View images and captions, and prepare a presentation.

Try This!
Complete activities and hands-on experiments.

AV² was built to bridge the gap between print and digital. We encourage you to tell us what you like and what you want to see in the future.

Sign up to be an AV² Ambassador at www.av2books.com/ambassador.

Due to the dynamic nature of the Internet, some of the URLs and activities provided as part of AV² by Weigl may have changed or ceased to exist. AV² by Weigl accepts no responsibility for any such changes. All media enhanced books are regularly monitored to update addresses and sites in a timely manner. Contact AV² by Weigl at 1-866-649-3445 or av2books@weigl.com with any questions, comments, or feedback.